A People in Focus Book

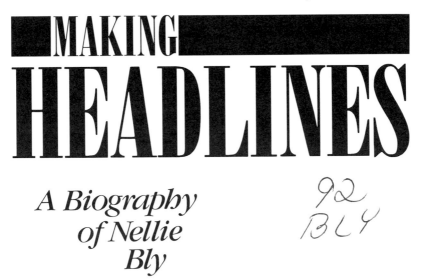

MAKING
HEADLINES

*A Biography
of Nellie
Bly*

**Kathy Lynn
Emerson**

DILLON PRESS, INC.
Minneapolis, Minnesota 55415

To my mother
Theresa Marie Coburg Gorton
who was born on Nellie Bly's birthday

Photographic Acknowledgments

The photographs have been reproduced through the courtesy of the Carnegie Library of Pittsburgh; the Historical Society of Western Pennsylvania; the Library of Congress; the National Archives; the New-York Historical Society, New York City; the New York Public Library, New York City; and UPI/Bettmann Newsphotos.

Library of Congress Cataloging-in-Publication Data

Emerson, Kathy Lynn.
  Making headlines : a biography of Nellie Bly / Kathy Lynn Emerson.
      p.   cm. — (A People in focus book)
  Bibliography: p.
  Includes index.
  Summary: Traces the life and achievements of the reporter/reformer who pursued a career in journalism at a time when such a career was not proper for a woman.
  ISBN 0-87518-406-5

  1. Bly, Nellie, 1867-1922—Biography—Juvenile literature. 2. Journalists—United States—Biography—Juvenile literature. [1. Bly, Nellie, 1867-1922. 2. Journalists.] I. Title. II. Series.
PN4874.C59E44   1989
070'.92'4—dc 19
[B]   88-35910
                                                                        CIP
                                                                        AC

Dillon Press, Inc., 242 Portland Avenue South
Minneapolis, Minnesota 55415

Printed in the United States of America
   2 3 4 5 6 7 8 9 10 98 97 96 95 94 93 92 91 90

Contents

Chapter/One

Every Bit a Lady

Who *is* this Nellie Bly?

That was the question people were asking from the moment the mysterious writer's name first appeared in a Pennsylvania newspaper, the Pittsburg *Dispatch*, in 1885.

The article said people should have the right to get a divorce. In the nineteenth century, that was a controversial opinion. No wonder the readers wondered about the author.

It can't be a real name, they said—it's a pen name like Mark Twain or Fanny Fern. The writer must have borrowed it from Stephen Foster's verses, since Nelly Bly is a character in one of his songs.

It can't be a woman, declared a great many

Nellie Bly as a young newspaperwoman.

men. Everyone knows women aren't capable of writing that well, and they don't have logical minds.
Obviously, the article was written by a man using a
woman's name.

No one guessed the truth. It was not a man who
stirred up all this fuss, and it was not the middle-
aged women's rights activist in bloomers that others
imagined, either. Nellie Bly was just eighteen years
old, and she was a lady.

In the 1880s there were dozens of rules for
ladylike behavior. A lady, girls were told, had her
name in the newspaper only three times in her life—
when she was born, when she married, and when
she died. A lady did not call attention to herself
by trying to invade territory men had staked out
as their own. She was not to think of becoming a
doctor or a lawyer, or of visiting an office, club,
or tavern.

At the same time, however, women who believed they were just as good as men had begun
to organize against the old ways. They did go to
college and obtain jobs. They spoke out in public,
and even dared ask for the right to vote. The wom-
en's suffrage movement had begun to gain strength.

Nellie Bly was not a suffragette; she never ac-
tively worked for women's rights. What she did was
quieter. She paved the way for future generations of

women in journalism, challenging them, by example, to make successful careers for themselves in the newspaper world.

Nellie Bly is best remembered for her trip around the world as a newspaper reporter—a journey that beat the speed record of Jules Verne's fictional character, Phileas Fogg. By 1890, anyone with luck and determination could have broken Fogg's eighty-day record. Nellie Bly received more attention during this trip than a man would have because it was very unusual for a woman—especially a charming, ladylike woman—to be so daring.

Determination was one of Nellie's trademarks from the beginning, as was being secretive about her private life. As a result, most of her childhood is a mystery. Even her true date of birth is not known. In later years she said she was eighteen when she first walked into a newspaper office. If so, she was born in 1867, but other records show she was born in 1865.

Nellie Bly started life with the name Elizabeth Cochran. She was born in Pitts Mills, Pennsylvania, just northeast of today's Pittsburgh. Except for one year at a boarding school, she was educated at home by her father, Michael Cochran. He was a self-made man, and his independent spirit greatly influenced his young daughter.

Nellie was born Elizabeth Cochran in this house in Cochran's Mills, Pennsylvania.

Cochran started out as a laborer and mill-worker. Then he bought the mill where he worked and all the land around the big farmhouse that was the family home. Eventually he owned so much land that he changed the name of the town to Cochran's Mills. He was the postmaster for a time, and a justice of the peace, and finally became associate judge of Armstrong County.

Elizabeth's mother, Mary Jane Kennedy, was Mr. Cochran's second wife. She stayed at home, raised her stepsons and her own children, kept house, and dressed her daughter in pink gingham dresses that earned Elizabeth the nickname Pinky.

Elizabeth's family eventually included ten children. She had three brothers of her own and three half brothers. In a family with so many boys, Pinky Cochran developed a fiercely independent spirit. She fought hard to "stand up to the boys," no matter how many times they challenged her. Yet as Pinky grew up, she learned to dress and act as a young lady did in that time and place.

In the nineteenth century, mothers taught their daughters to be ladies—and that meant dressing modestly. Skirts swept the ground, and blouses and jackets had long sleeves and high necklines trimmed with lace. Underneath were layers and layers of undergarments—only the most daring wore Amelia Bloomer's "bloomers," which were long, loose trousers. Ladies wore hats and gloves whenever they went out, which wasn't very often.

Since most establishments were for men only, there weren't many places for women to go. Ladies were supposed to stay at home, do needlepoint, and care for the children.

Girls were told that ladies did not use certain common words. They were not supposed to say "sweat" or even "perspire." A lady "glowed." A lady would not refer to legs—her own were hidden by her long skirt, and she was supposed to pretend they didn't exist. Also, she did not curse or use bad language of any kind.

Pinky Cochran was raised to be every bit a lady, but when her father died, she had more to think about than clothes and manners. A lady who had no father to support her had only three choices in the 1880s: to get married, to live as a poor relation on the handouts of another member of the family, or to find a way to earn money herself.

Soon after her father's death, Pinky Cochrane (she added the final *e* to her name) and her mother moved to Pittsburg, which did not add the final *h* until 1911. Mrs. Cochran wasn't used to fast-paced, expensive city life. Gradually, she spent almost all the money her husband had left the family, and there was barely enough left for food and shelter. Elizabeth Cochrane had little choice but to find a job, and she was determined to do so. The welfare of her family depended on it.

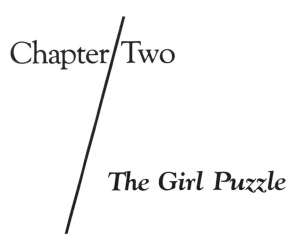

Chapter/Two

The Girl Puzzle

What Elizabeth Cochrane really wanted to do was write. A female writer was not a new idea in 1885; Louisa May Alcott had been earning a living as a novelist for nearly twenty years. Elizabeth had probably read *Little Women*. If she did, she knew that Alcott's character, Jo March, stormed a newspaper office to sell her stories.

Elizabeth may have heard tales of women who were newspaper reporters, too. By 1880, almost every major newspaper in the United States paid women to write feature articles, usually essays in letter form, and send them in through the mail. In New York City, a female writer who used the name Jenny June worked in a newspaper office on a day-to-day basis. Another young woman named Sally

Joy had talked herself into a job on the Boston *Post* when she was eighteen. Still, compared to New York, Pittsburg was a small place, and its people had old-fashioned ideas. Elizabeth might never have become a journalist if it hadn't been for a newspaper column titled "What Girls Are Good For."

This essay expressed ideas held by most men in the 1880s. The writer protested the alarming trend of hiring women to work in shops and offices, and called the employment of women in business a threat to the national welfare.

Other unfair, harshly critical remarks filled the column, too. When Elizabeth Cochrane read them, she became so angry that she sat down and wrote a letter to George A. Madden, managing editor of the Pittsburg *Dispatch*. She didn't use her name in the letter—that wouldn't have been ladylike. Instead, she signed it "Lonely Orphan Girl" and sent it off.

George Madden was so impressed by the letter that he wanted to find the author and hire him to work on the *Dispatch*. It never entered his mind that the writer might be a woman. He pictured the writer as a young man who wanted to work for the *Dispatch*, and had deliberately taken the wrong side of the issue to get attention.

On January 17, 1885, an advertisement appeared in the *Dispatch*, asking "Lonely Orphan

Girl" to contact Mr. Madden. Once more Elizabeth addressed a note to the editor, but this time she signed her own name. Mr. Madden may have groaned in dismay, imagining some old "battle-ax" with strong feminist views, but he wrote back anyway. She did, after all, write well. He said that he would be willing to consider publishing an article on "girls and their spheres in life" in the Sunday paper if she would write and submit it.

Elizabeth sent in the article as soon as she could get it written, and Madden liked it. He paid her five dollars, and published her work on January 25 under the title "The Girl Puzzle." Then, throwing caution to the wind, Madden wrote to Elizabeth once more to ask if she had any other suggestions for stories. He had no idea how she would respond, but the last thing he expected was that she would turn up several days later at the Fifth Street offices of the *Dispatch*.

Elizabeth Cochrane appeared fragile for her height of five feet five inches. She wore her chestnut-colored hair in a chignon with bangs, a youthful style in those days, and had a jaunty sailor hat on her head. In spite of the determined gleam in her wide hazel eyes, she had a meek and mild appearance. The *Dispatch*'s reporters, who shared the one big city room, didn't know what to think of her.

Newspaper offices in the nineteenth century echoed with the clatter of presses from the floors below. The rooms smelled of printers ink, gaslights, and tobacco, and were filled with a haze of cigar smoke. Chewing tobacco was popular, too, and the men were often careless when they aimed at the spittoons. The floors were filthy. In Sally Joy's city room in Boston, the more gentlemanly reporters put newspapers down so she wouldn't get her long skirts stained with tobacco juice.

Elizabeth Cochrane looked out of place in this setting. A more timid woman would have turned and fled, but her ladylike appearance masked a will of iron. She informed the gawking reporters, sitting at desks crowded together and piled high with copy paper, that Mr. Madden had sent for her. When they directed her to his desk, she introduced herself and said she had come with her ideas.

If George Madden was surprised by Elizabeth Cochrane's sudden appearance in his city room, he was shocked by the subject on which she wanted to write. Divorce, she told him, was an issue that needed to be discussed in the newspaper.

Elizabeth tried hard to persuade Mr. Madden to give her a chance. He protested at first, but finally agreed to let her prove she could do what she said she could. He sent her home to write her article on

In the nineteenth century, newspaper offices such as this one were not considered proper places for a young lady to work.

divorce, and probably thought he would never see her again.

Elizabeth, however, tackled her new project immediately. She had the notes on divorce cases that her father had made during his years as a judge, but she had been doing some research of her own as well. Since she and her mother had spent almost all of their inheritance from her father, they had changed addresses several times, each time selecting a less expensive place. By the time "What Girls Are Good For" was printed, they were living in run-down lodgings in a poor section of the city, where

Elizabeth had talked to several women who had suffered because of unfair divorce laws.

All night long, Elizabeth worked on her article, writing and revising, scratching out passages and copying it over. At that time there were no word processors and no portable typewriters to make the work easier. Even in the newspaper offices, articles were composed with pen and ink. Despite the long, slow process, Elizabeth persisted until her story was just the way she wanted it. The next morning she returned to the *Dispatch* office with a final draft that was neat and easy to read. More importantly, the article said something. Mr. Madden was impressed and immediately agreed to publish the story.

George Madden was a businessman. He might have believed, as the article in his paper had said, that respectable women stayed at home until they married, or at worse went into a "woman's profession" such as teaching or nursing. Still, he knew the facts. Since the Civil War, women had been working in mills, factories, and offices. The thought of a woman in politics made him shudder, but a woman had run for president in 1884.

In spite of his doubts, Madden found himself encouraging Elizabeth Cochrane. If one thing could overcome his prejudices, it was the promise of a controversial series for his newspaper. Controversy increased a newspaper's circulation, and that was good business.

He asked for more stories, saying that if the series on divorce were a success, he would give Elizabeth a regular job and pay her five dollars a week. She accepted at once.

Madden had only one problem left. He was worried about allowing Elizabeth to use her own name. What would people say if they knew he had hired an eighteen-year-old girl to write on such a sensitive subject as divorce? What would her family say? She had respectable and old-fashioned older brothers who would not approve of her new career.

Just as Mr. Madden and Elizabeth Cochrane agreed to invent a pen name, Mr. Madden's assistant, Erasmus Wilson, began to hum a popular Stephen Foster song. Everyone knew the words:

> Nelly Bly, Nelly Bly,
> bring the broom along.
> We'll sweep the kitchen clear, my dear,
> and have a little song.
> Poke the wood, my lady love,
> and make the fire burn,
> And while I take the banjo down,
> just give the mush a turn.
> Heigh, Nelly, Ho, Nelly,
> listen love, to me;
> I'll sing for you, play for you,
> a dulcet melody.

From that day on, Elizabeth Cochrane was Nellie Bly, and Madden immediately published her articles on divorce. The subject alone was enough to make people sit up and take notice, but the newspaper-reading public of Pittsburg was just as intrigued by the author. Who was this Nellie Bly? they wondered.

The *Dispatch* made the most of the mystery surrounding its new reporter's identity. Circulation improved dramatically as Nellie wrote more articles. In time, she came up with an idea that would set the tone for her entire newspaper career—she asked Mr. Madden if she could write about life in the slums and factories of Pittsburg. As a reporter and a reformer, she would tell the real story of her own experiences visiting these places, from a lady's point of view. She would take an artist with her to sketch what she saw. Mr. Madden saw the circulation of the *Dispatch* going up and up...and agreed.

Chapter/Three

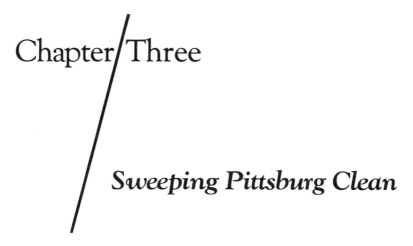

Sweeping Pittsburg Clean

Nellie brought the broom along, as the song says, and set out to sweep Pittsburg clean. It needed it. Under smoke-blackened skies, which glowed flame red at night, workers were little more than slaves to uncaring factory owners. Women in a bottle factory worked fourteen-hour days in an unheated building. Children were endangered by living in dirty, disease-ridden, fire-prone buildings in a slum called the Point.

When Nellie Bly joined the staff of the *Dispatch*, more than 156,000 people lived in Pittsburg. Many were immigrants, drawn by jobs in the iron and steel industries. Few labor unions protected these unskilled workers, and no social service agencies existed.

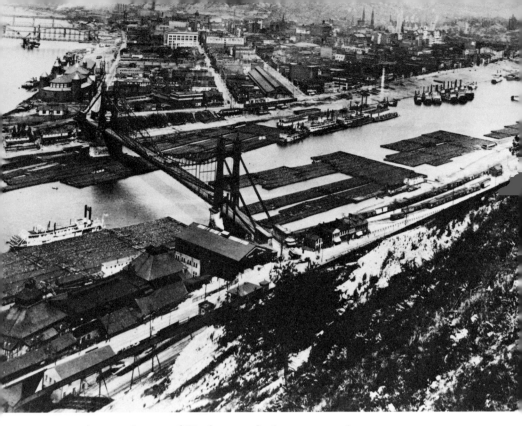

An aerial view of Pittsburg in the late nineteenth century.

Nellie brought her discoveries of social injustices to public attention through the *Dispatch*. She was not content to sit at her hard-won desk in the city room, letting others do the research. Every story was her own, from the first idea, through the investigation and writing, to her byline, or name, on the finished article.

A bottling factory was Nellie's first target. The glass industry was Pittsburg's third largest business; some seventy factories produced half the nation's glass, and more champagne bottles than there were in France. Accompanied by her artist, she located

Women working in a Pittsburg bottling factory in the early 1890s.

the factory owner and told him she wanted to write an article for the *Dispatch* about his factory. Deceived by her ladylike manner and pleasant smile, he welcomed her with open arms. He thought she was offering him good, free publicity, so he told her to talk to anyone and look anywhere.

Nellie talked to the workers as the artist sketched. Some of these women stood on an icy cement floor for fourteen hours at a stretch. To cope with the winter cold that seeped through the factory walls, the workers had to wrap rags around their feet, which kept their toes from freezing.

Several hundred workers shared one toilet, along with a family of rats. Worse yet was the daily risk of injury from broken or exploding bottles. Since worker's compensation did not exist, an injury could result in the loss of a person's job and only source of income.

Nellie was shocked by the conditions in the factories, and she channeled all her outrage into print. She held nothing back, including names, dates, and drawings. When her article appeared in the *Dispatch*, every copy of that day's paper sold quickly at the city's newsstands.

The factory owners were enraged when they saw Nellie's articles. Letters flooded the *Dispatch* office. Although Nellie faced protests, and even threats, efforts at reform began which eventually improved conditions in the factories of Pittsburg.

Nellie attacked the slums next. In the course of her own frequent moves, she had seen how crowded many of the city's tenement buildings were. In the Point she found a family of twelve living in one unheated room. In the rickety wooden shanties along Yellow Row, and the ramshackle cottages on the hill at Skunk Hollow, Nellie Bly asked questions and got answers. When she wrote her story, she named the slumlords, hoping to shame them into repairing their buildings.

Nellie reported on crowded living conditions in the Point, a Pittsburg slum.

The uproar this time was even greater than it had been after her article about the factory. Pittsburg businessmen began to organize against the threat of Nellie Bly. They claimed she was ruining the city's reputation. Despite fourteen thousand chimneys that polluted the air, they still insisted that Pittsburg was one of the healthiest cities in the United States. In fact, they said that people worked so hard that they didn't notice the smoke. Pollution had killed the grass and flowers, but a child who complained about the foulness of the air was told she should be "grateful for God's goodness in

making work, which made smoke, which made prosperity." With that kind of thinking, no wonder the businessmen threatened George Madden with the loss of all his advertising if he didn't stop those reform-minded articles by Nellie Bly.

George Madden's business sense told him it was time to let things cool down. He gave Nellie a raise to ten dollars a week and made her society editor for the *Dispatch*. Nellie Bly began writing about the upper classes, whose parties, art, drama, and books were part of a world far removed from the city's slums.

Plays, lectures, concerts, and charity balls soon left Nellie bored and restless. "I was too impatient," she wrote, "to work along at the usual duties assigned women on newspapers." Yet nearly a year passed before she could persuade Mr. Madden to let her write serious articles again.

A modern jail, Riverside Penitentiary of Western Pennsylvania, had just been built to replace the old Western Penitentiary. It was the most up-to-date facility of its kind, and Nellie wanted to visit it. Her article would be full of praise, she argued. Why not let her cover its opening? Reluctantly, Madden agreed.

In her article, Nellie praised the new facility's separate cells for inmates and large common work

The run-down tenement houses of Pittsburg's Yellow Row were another of Nellie's targets.

and recreation areas, but she used this praise of one jail as a starting point to criticize the rest. When Madden read her attack on other Pennsylvania jails, he knew trouble lay ahead, but he decided to print the article anyway.

Meanwhile, Nellie wanted to take another look at the factories. This time she went undercover, dressing herself as a poor woman looking for a job. She was hired at the first factory where she applied, though she had no skills. Her job was to hitch cables together in an assembly line with other young women. They could be fined for talking, or even for smiling, but Nellie did manage to learn that they all suffered from headaches.

She soon understood why. The light was so dim that her head began to ache, too. Then her feet started to hurt, because she had to stand. Her hands became raw and started to bleed. Before long, she ached all over. Just like the workers in the bottle factory, these young women kept working in spite of their fear of blindness and the constant discomfort. They had to work to live.

The women's supervisor kept urging them to work faster and faster. He paced back and forth behind them, yelling out threats and foul language. Since Nellie had been brought up to have good manners, she found it difficult to listen to curses and insults for hours on end. Finally, Nellie simply walked away from the assembly line to get a drink of water. The foreman fired her.

When Nellie's two stories appeared in the *Dispatch*, the response was overwhelming. The paper's sales increased, and Nellie was criticized by just about everyone. City law enforcement officials said she wasn't qualified to judge their jails. The clergy called her shameless for visiting a men's prison without a chaperon. Again, the factory owners and businessmen of Pittsburg threatened to withdraw their advertising. Madden raised Nellie's pay to fifteen dollars a week and sent her back to write the society page.

The other reporters of the *Dispatch* appreciated her, even if the targets of her articles didn't. "Only a few months previous I had become a newspaper woman," she wrote, and in October 1886, she became the first woman invited to join the Pittsburg Press Club. She was not, however, given any more controversial assignments.

Then one day, Nellie Bly saw a picture of some Aztec ruins in an art gallery window. Suddenly, story ideas about Mexico tumbled one after another into her mind. Nellie believed she could write articles describing what she saw, as travelogues did, but she could add more substance to her stories.

As usual, Nellie's enthusiastic plans didn't impress her boss at the *Dispatch*. She couldn't go running off to Mexico alone, Madden protested. Mexico had an unstable government. Mexicans mistrusted foreign reporters, and she didn't even speak Spanish.

Nellie had an answer for everything. She would learn Spanish and travel with her mother. What could be more respectable? she asked. Besides, she would not be going as a reporter for the *Dispatch*— the trip to Mexico would be a personal vacation. Of course, if Mr. Madden wanted to buy any stories, she would be sending some back....

Chapter/Four

A Second Columbus

"One wintry night," Nellie wrote, "I bade my few journalistic friends adieu, and, accompanied by my mother, started on my way to Mexico."

As their train was approaching El Paso, Texas, Mrs. Cochran climbed out of her berth and looked through the curtains. "It's so dark!" she exclaimed in dismay. "What shall we do when we arrive?"

"I'm glad it's dark," Nellie told her cheerfully, "because I won't have to button my boots or comb my hair."

When they left the train, though, they discovered that there were no porters, no cabs, and no hotels. The other passengers were staying at the train station for the rest of the night to wait for the next day's train to Mexico City. The dim light of one oil lamp showed Nellie and her mother a dismal waiting room packed with men, women, children, dogs, and baggage. Some people were asleep. Others were drinking, smoking, and playing cards.

"This has taught me a lesson," Nellie joked. She declared she would fall into the arms of the first man who mentioned the word "marry" to her so that she would have someone to look after her. In reality, no one needed looking after less than Nellie Bly. She spoke only a little Spanish, but it was enough. She soon found a house where she and her mother could stay for the night.

Finally, Nellie and her mother arrived in Mexico City, where they found lodgings in a private home. Nellie said she only missed Pennsylvania at mealtimes, but her mother had a more difficult time. The Mexican food made her ill, and the strange sights and sounds frightened her. She was terribly homesick, and soon she was begging Nellie to take her home. Instead, Nellie put her mother on a northbound train alone—and stayed in Mexico.

As she had in Pittsburg, Nellie learned of the poverty, overcrowding, and homelessness in this foreign land. Yet she also wrote about fashions, festivals, and horseback riding. She visited museums and tombs and ruins and learned enough Mexican history to write letters home to her paper,

Nellie as she appeared about the time of her journey to Mexico.

the *Dispatch*, about what she had seen. Nellie also attended carnivals and theater performances, and studied the customs and opinions of those she observed.

Knowing her readers would be interested in courtship and marriage among the Mexicans, Nellie investigated this subject. "You would naturally wonder," she wrote, "how a girl who never leaves her mother's or chaperon's side, who never goes to parties, who is watched like a condemned murderess, would ever get a lover; but notwithstanding all this strictness they number less old maids and more admirers than their sisters in the States."

In Mexico City, Nellie Bly met Joaquin Miller, a middle-aged American poet visiting from California. This bearded intellectual, famous for his belief in living the simple life, became a close friend. Once, in her travels around the city, she discovered a street entirely populated by coffin makers. Knowing this was exactly the sort of oddity Miller loved, she took him there. His praise was music to her ears. "Little Nell," he told her, "you are a second Columbus. You have discovered a street that has no like in the world, and I have been over the world twice."

These exciting words made Nellie Bly think of wider travels. First, she wanted to see as much of the Mexican countryside as she could. Wherever the railroads went, so did Nellie Bly.

On a trip to Jalapa, Nellie took a streetcar. Her presence aboard without a male escort created quite a stir. Everyone stared at her. "But," she wrote later, "I defied their gaze and showed them that a free American girl can accommodate herself to circumstances without the aid of a man."

Nellie knew how to stand up for herself. Later in the same trip, when she prepared to pay for her room, she discovered that she had been charged for two days instead of one. "I did not know the Spanish word for cheat," Nellie admitted, "but I wanted to get as near it as possible."

Nellie decided that in the future she wouldn't even drink a glass of water until she knew the price. This precaution was not only for herself, but for all Americans. She did not intend to allow a "Yankee girl to be cheated."

In many ways, Nellie was the "ugly American" type of tourist. She hadn't troubled to learn much about Mexico before she went, and when she was confused or offended, she tended to condemn. Overall, her portrait of Mexico was not a flattering one.

Nellie Bly was particularly upset about the corrupt practices of the Mexican government. Even worse in her opinion, no one dared criticize the system—least of all the Mexican newspapers. When she sent the *Dispatch* a story about some editors who had been put in jail, the article was picked up by other U.S. newspapers and reprinted. Soon afterward, her article came to the attention of the Mexican government, and Nellie had good reason to be worried.

"I had some regard for my health," Nellie wrote, "and a Mexican jail is the least desirable abode on the face of the earth." An American prisoner in a Mexican jail was given just two meals a week—"not enough to sustain life in a sick cat." There were no beds and no water, and prisoners lived in constant fear that the jailers would shoot them in the back if they caused trouble.

Knowing that "secret police" now followed her wherever she went, Nellie devised a plan for transporting her notes for future stories back to the United States. Her first step was to buy large amounts of gaudy lingerie—in plain sight of the secret agent who was following her. Then, at the train station, she turned to the agent, smiled in a friendly way, and asked if he would help her with her baggage. Would he be too much of a gentleman to go through her lingerie? Or would he search the suitcases anyway? she wondered.

Making the best of the embarrassing situation, the agent escorted her to a seat on the train and told the conductor that she was not to be searched or delayed. Nellie's plan worked, and the journalist's notes reached El Paso safely, hidden in the suitcase with her underwear.

After she returned from Mexico, Pittsburg seemed too small for her. Nellie Bly's stories from Mexico were being published all over America. Her public wanted more, perhaps even a book. It was time to go to New York.

Chapter/Five

Prisoner at Blackwell's Island

July of 1887 in New York City was hot and humid. Nellie Bly had a tiny, furnished attic room in a brownstone building on Lexington Avenue, an arrangement with a syndicate, or publishing group, to print the rest of her stories about Mexico, sixty-five dollars she had saved from her work at the *Dispatch*, and the cocky self-confidence of a twenty year old. She had no doubt that she would find a position at one of the many newspaper offices on Park Row.

As the uncomfortable summer turned into an equally hot fall, however, she had to accept the hard truth. New York City had many talented newspaper reporters, and no one thought Nellie Bly was anybody special. She couldn't even get past the office boys to talk to an editor.

Joseph Pulitzer, the publisher of the New York World.

The final straw came when her pocketbook, which contained all her money, was stolen in Central Park. Now, no time was left for writing letters or sending in resumes. She had to have a job, and she had to have one quickly.

Nellie knew which New York newspaper she most wanted to work for—the *World*, published by Joseph Pulitzer. He was a reformer, as Nellie was, and he had the kind of flair she appreciated. A year earlier, he had singlehandedly raised enough money to construct a base for the Statue of Liberty by using a sketch of the statue in the masthead of the

Evening World and by publishing the names of everyone who donated money.

Nellie had written to Pulitzer during the summer, offering to participate in a balloon flight he
was sponsoring from Saint Louis, Missouri, but a
male reporter had been selected to go instead. Now
she was determined to contact Mr. Pulitzer again,
in person this time, and convince him to give her
a job.

The gold-domed World building had broad
steps leading to a small, dark lobby. Nellie had
reached that point before. Now she stood at the low
gate and railing that separated the lobby from the
offices beyond and told the office boy she intended
to wait right there until Mr. Pulitzer agreed to see
her. She had put him in an awkward position, and
she knew it. Because she was obviously a lady, he
couldn't throw her out of the building. On the
other hand, he didn't dare brave Mr. Pulitzer's
wrath by letting her in.

Joseph Pulitzer suffered from a number of ail-
ments. He was almost blind, and both light and
noise bothered him intensely. His office at the
World was specially designed to lessen his discomfort. He was also convinced that rival publishers
were spying on him. No one dared disturb him with
the news that Nellie Bly was below.

The World building in New York City, home of the newspaper Nellie was determined to work for.

Three hours passed. Pulitzer's reporters began to notice what was going on, and they discussed what ought to be done about the intruder. Nellie watched for her chance, and when no one was looking, she slipped through the gate. Boldly, she climbed three flights of stairs to the wide, carpeted hall that led to the offices of both Pulitzer and his managing editor, John Cockerill. Nellie was pursued by the panic-stricken office boy. Finally, rather than let her walk in unannounced, he opened the door and introduced her. "She don't give up easy," he added as he fled.

In the office were both Pulitzer and Cockerill. Nellie had their undivided attention and made good use of it. She had brought her clippings from the *Dispatch*, and she had also brought ideas for newspaper stories. In spite of their annoyance at being interrupted, the two men listened. One proposal in particular caught their interest.

Nellie wanted to pretend to be insane in order to be committed to the mental hospital on Blackwell's Island. Then she would write an article about the living conditions there. Another reporter, Julius Chambers, had tackled a similar assignment back in 1872 when he spent ten days in Bloomingdale Asylum and wrote about his experiences for the *Tribune*. The articles had been very popular. Pulitzer saw a chance to use the same stunt in a bigger and better way. He gave Nellie twenty-five dollars for the idea, and promised to decide within three days if the paper would hire her to carry it out.

What followed was one of the most sensational, and dangerous, adventures of Nellie's career. She planned every move carefully, until the point when she would actually be committed as insane. After that she would have to rely on Mr. Pulitzer to get her out of the asylum.

"I am in a fit mood for my mission and come what may I am determined not to shirk," she wrote as she began. She left her room on a Monday morning, telling her landlady she would be away a few days, and went to a cheap lodging house on Second Avenue called the Temporary Home for Females. Although she had dressed respectably, Nellie took only seventy-three cents with her. She told the matron, Mrs. Stanard, that her name was Nellie Brown and that she had just arrived from Cuba. She even threw in a few sentences of her newly acquired Spanish. After paying thirty cents for a night's lodging, Nellie went to her room. At supper, she began her act.

The lodgers were frightened by this strange girl's crying and shaking. She fought them when they tried to put her to bed, and asked for her pistol, which she said they had stolen from her. Finally, the matron bundled her off to the Essex Market Police Station. Newspaper reporters were called in to try to identify her, but Nellie played her role well. No one recognized her as Nellie Bly. She pretended to have lost her memory, and spoke more Spanish than English. A judge, a policeman, and finally a doctor all thought she was seriously disturbed, and sent her to Bellevue "insane pavilion" by ambulance.

Though she was excited and pleased by her success, she began to be frightened. In Bellevue she was put in a ward with three other "insane" women who acted quite sane. When a doctor finally came to question her, he didn't seem to care if she were mentally ill or not. He just wanted to know if she were a prostitute!

Later, a newspaper reporter came to interview Nellie Brown, and Nellie overheard the nurse turn him away. "She's a hopeless case," the nurse said.

Nellie was kept as a prisoner for several days, and then, on September 25, 1887, faced the panel of doctors who were to decide her fate. Bravely, she played her role. The doctors declared that she was suffering from "dementia with delusions of persecution" and sentenced her to the Blackwell's Island mental hospital.

From then on, Nellie's treatment went from bad to worse, starting with the ambulance attendant who tried to kiss her on the way to the East River wharf. The Blackwell's Island barge was filthy, and the matrons horrible to see. When the boat docked, one told her, grinning, "You'll never get out of here, dearie. Never."

Other New York newspapers ran the Nellie Brown story, but not the *World*. "Who is this insane girl?" Pulitzer's biggest rival asked, describing her as "a modest, comely, well-dressed girl of nineteen." One *Sun* reporter thought he had solved the mystery, identifying the mystery woman as Lottie Peters, someone who had disappeared in New Orleans, Louisiana.

Meanwhile, on Blackwell's Island, Nellie was having serious second thoughts. Now that it was too late, now that she was totally dependent upon Joseph Pulitzer for rescue, she wondered if she had been too bold. She was examined again, weighing in at 112 pounds. She told the doctor she was not sick and did not want to stay. He ignored her.

There were abuses in every aspect of life on Blackwell's Island. The inmates were fed poorly, while the nurses ate good cuts of meat, white bread, and fresh fruit. The prisoners took baths in a bare, unheated room in an iron tub. Everyone used the same water, shared a dirty towel, and wore only a thin flannel slip when they were sent, still dripping, back to the wards. It didn't matter that some of the women were ill, or that some had lice. When Nellie protested, she was put in solitary confinement for the night.

It rained for five days while Nellie was on Blackwell's Island. The inmates had nothing to do but sit in a reception room all day long. Though talking and moving about were forbidden, Nellie managed to speak to many of the women. She was shocked and frightened to realize that she was not the only one there who was sane.

"From the moment I entered the insane ward of the Island," she later wrote, "I made no attempt to keep up the role of insanity. I talked and acted just as I do in ordinary life. Yet, strange to say, the more sanely I talked and acted, the crazier I was thought to be...." When she asked to be examined to prove she had recovered, she was refused, and when she insisted, the nurses reported that she was "raving."

Ten days passed before the *World* sent a lawyer to get "Nellie Brown" off of Blackwell's Island. "I was overjoyed," Nellie wrote. "The Insane Asylum on Blackwell's Island is a human rat trap. It is easy to get in, but once there, it is impossible to get out."

On Saturday, October 8, 1887, the front page of the *World* ran an ad: "The Mysterious Girl Who Puzzled the Doctors at Bellevue—See The Sunday World." "Behind Asylum Bars," the first install- ment of Nellie's adventures, took up almost an en- tire page, and extra copies of that edition had to be printed. As a result of Nellie's articles, she won a full-time job on Pulitzer's staff, and her own desk at the *World.* Even the *Sun* had to admit the stories were remarkable. "Nellie Bly Too Sharp for Island Doctors," heralded its headlines. Newspapers all over the country picked up the story, and soon the name Nellie Bly was known everywhere.

Investigations of Blackwell's Island by the Board of Charities began at once. When Nellie was invited back to the island, she found that in only twenty days changes had already occurred. Some were at- tempts to cover up what had been going on, but eventually officials admitted she had been right and thanked her for her courageous reporting.

The superintendent, Dr. Dent, decided to in- form the public about the problems of running the institution. As a result of his efforts and Nellie's articles, a grand jury investigated the asylum. Nel- lie's particular friends among the inmates were re-evaluated, and, as Nellie proudly wrote, "the Grand Jury's report to the court advised all the changes I had proposed." Thousands of dollars were set aside to improve Blackwell's Island and other asylums.

Nellie Bly was not yet twenty-one, but she had everything she wanted—a job, fame, and a reading audience that was eager to see what she would write about next. She did not keep them waiting long.

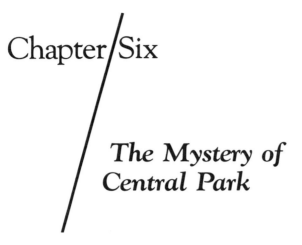

Chapter Six

The Mystery of Central Park

Nellie Bly's picture disappeared from the *World* for a long time. Joseph Pulitzer realized that Nellie's ability to go anywhere and pretend to be anyone was an advantage for the kind of story she wanted to write. He assigned her to work under Mr. Goddard, editor of the *Sunday World*, but Nellie still chose her own topics and went about gathering information in her own way.

Her first targets were the employment services, which claimed to help poor immigrant women find jobs. Although the Statue of Liberty had been erected in New York Harbor to welcome people to America's shores, no laws existed to protect the newcomers once they arrived in America.

Nellie went to the Germania Servant's Agency

Nellie during the time she wrote for the World.

on Fourth Avenue in October 1887. Before she could open her mouth, she was asked to pay a registration fee. Then the owner told her that because she was a "nice looking girl," he would rent her living space in his own quarters behind the agency. Then he found her a job as a laundress, although she had no qualifications. The second agency was no better, nor any of the others she visited.

Nellie Bly's article called for laws to protect both the employer and the worker. "She has no references; the agent knows nothing of her character; nevertheless he declares she possesses all the virtues on the calendar." A common thief, she pointed out, could easily find a job in any of New York's finest homes with the aid of an employment agency.

Nellie's next targets were New York's factories. The most dangerous factory jobs were those in soap packing, which involved working with dangerous chemicals; flower making, which used arsenic; and tobacco stripping. A smart working woman learned to avoid "Homes for Females," and advertisements that guaranteed "steady work." Everywhere, people were trying to exploit these newcomers to New York.

Nellie wrote about the tremendous struggle the female newcomers had just to stay alive and keep a roof over their heads. She admired them greatly, pointing out that these "white slaves" were often better people than women she had seen "in high positions" in New York society.

Nellie Bly was such a talented reporter that she was selected to take on a dangerous assignment for the New York *World*—the exposure of a corrupt lobbyist, Edward R. Phelps, a man who tried to influence government officials to pass certain laws. Everyone knew Phelps was bribing members of the New York State Assembly, but no one had any proof. Nellie pretended to be Mrs. Brown, the wife of a man in the patent medicine business who wanted Bill 191, the Smith Patent Medicine Bill, defeated.

In late March 1888, Nellie entered Room 98 of the Kenmore Hotel in Albany, New York, and saw the man known as the "King of the Lobby." He was not what she had expected. "This self-possessed, smiling man could not be the vampire I had been made to believe him," she wrote.

"Mr. Phelps," Nellie said, "I came to consult you on a matter of importance. I hope no one can overhear us?"

"Oh, no," he assured her, "you are safe to speak here." He drew his chair closer to her and gave her a pleasant smile.

Nellie Bly thought Bill 191 was a good one because it protected people from quack medicines. But as Mrs. Brown, she pretended it would ruin her husband's business. "Do you think you could kill it?" she asked.

"Oh, yes," Phelps said. "Never fear. I'll have it killed." Then he added, "It will take money, you know."

Nellie clutched at her umbrella and said, "I am willing to pay anything up to $2,000 if you will assure me that it will be stopped."

"I can assure you that, of course. You don't need to talk of $2,000. You see, there will be my expenses, and then I will have to pay some Assemblymen." He showed her twelve names. One was "a rich man, and can't be bought," he told her, but he put check marks next to the names who could— Gallagher, Tallmadge, Prime, DeWitt, Hagan, and McLoughlin.

"How much will it take for them?" she asked.

"You can get the lot for $1,000."

Nellie made arrangements to meet Phelps in New York City the following Friday to conclude the deal. She even got the list of names away from him—proof of the conspiracy.

The second meeting, in New York, almost led to Nellie's exposure. Phelps wanted a check from her, and she did not have it. Finally, she convinced him to let her go to her hotel and meet him there later. Instead, she went to the *World* office.

The front page of the *Sunday World* on April 1 carried the headline, "Edward R. Phelps Caught in a Neatly Laid Trap." Next to the headline was a cartoon of Phelps, surrounded by bags of money. Phelps denied everything, including the existence of Nellie Bly, but on April 18, at 4 P.M., she appeared in Albany to testify before the House Judiciary Committee. "After she was finished," the *World* reported, "there was not the slightest doubt in the minds of all honest men of the accuracy of her statements and the truth."

After this court appearance, Nellie had to have a bodyguard in Albany, but it was not only the crooked politicians who were angry with her. Her fellow reporters were upset, too—some of them didn't think a woman should have had such an important assignment.

Nellie went back to "women's stories" after that, but they were no less dangerous. First she took on the free clinics, where the poor went for medical aid. Instead of providing cures, these clinics actually spread disease. They were run by young, inexperienced, unsupervised doctors. To prove that patients of the free clinic were treated without any real concern for their health, Nellie had to let herself be examined. The doctor did not, she reported, even clean his instruments between patients!

Letters came to the *World* addressed to Nellie Bly, telling her about situations that needed to be investigated. That was how she heard about a man who preyed on young women he found walking in Central Park. "Nellie Bly," the letter writer asked, "can't you find out something about him?" She went after the story the only way she knew how— by using herself as bait.

"How about a little ride, girlie?" the driver of an open carriage called down to her. "It's a swell day for a drive and I have good horses. Come on, let's have some fun."

He was not good-looking, Nellie reported. His collar was soiled, and his chin was covered with stubble. He had a long, drooping mustache and hair that hung low over his forehead.

After a bit of conversation, Nellie pretended to be interested when he said he could get her on the stage as an actress. He said his name was Charlie and that he had a friend who owned a roadhouse. After a short ride, he brought her back to the park bench where he had found her and asked if he would see her the next day. "I can't," she told him, "but I'll be here the day after."

Meanwhile, Nellie got help from the *World* staff. A photographer got a picture of Charlie, and another reporter followed him to the livery stable and found out that his last name was Cleveland. Although this was a start, the hard part still lay ahead. Nellie had to get into Charles Cleveland's carriage again.

This time he drove her to the roadhouse he had told her about, and there he tried to get her to drink some sherry. Then he wanted her to sing for him, saying he would get her a job at a summer resort.

"I don't intend to sing," Nellie told him. "I want to be driven back to the park. I should think you'd get into trouble, going around picking up girls like this."

"Not me. It's the girls who get into trouble. And if I have any fuss with them I tip off the police and the girls get hauled in—to jail."

"You mean girls—that I myself—might get put in jail if I don't do what you ask?"

Cleveland laughed at her. "I know what I'm doing," he bragged. "I watch for strangers. I knew you were a stranger when I first saw you. I drive in that park all the time and I know when a strange girl comes into it."

"I'm not as friendless as you seem to think," Nellie said, and demanded he drive her to the park.

Nellie, determined, was hard to refuse. He did as she asked. The next day her story ran three columns under the headline "The Infamy of the Park." Unsuspecting girls were warned. Charles Cleveland disappeared and was never heard of again. At police headquarters, several members of the force were suspended. Later, in 1889, Nellie wrote a novel, *The Mystery of Central Park*, based on her adventures.

Since Cleveland had said it was easy to send innocent women to jail, Nellie Bly decided to investigate his claim. Early in 1889, Nellie arranged to have herself arrested. With a friend who called herself Miss Peters, Nellie registered at the Gedney House. Then her friend claimed that Nellie had taken two fifty-dollar bills from her purse. The police were called, and Nellie was arrested, searched, and put in a cell.

As she listened to the conversations around her, a lawyer approached her. He said he could get her out with the help of McClelland, an influential politician who was easily bribed. Nellie declined the lawyer's offer. "I am innocent, so I am not afraid."

"They have got a case against you for sure," he insisted. "The woman whose money is missing is out there with two witnesses. But you give me ten dollars and McClelland will make everything all right."

"I'll think it over," Nellie said.

"If you don't, I'll be out there beside you and I'll see that you're put under a thousand dollars' bail. The Grand Jury will get you then."

Nellie knew that no witnesses would appear against her, and she would be released. Still, she was angry when she thought about all the women this lawyer had frightened into paying him. Her story exposed him, but she was kind to those who had treated her well. Nellie wrote that matrons should do the searching at police stations, and urged that male and female prisoners be separated. She also wrote that "innocent women falling into the hands of the police are not necessarily badly treated. If all the turnkeys are as kind as the one I encountered, no women could ever fill their places."

Because of Nellie Bly, improvements were made in factories, clinics, and police stations throughout the city. Nellie was not afraid to risk her own health and safety to win needed reforms. From the moment she began work for the *World*, she was a crusader, but there was a lighter side to her writing, too. There was even time, once in a while, for a personal life.

Chapter/Seven

Nellie Bly on the Stage

"Please won't you tell me if you are a man or a woman?" a letter asked Nellie in May 1887, when she was still with the Pittsburg *Dispatch*. "My husband's brother says you never existed at all and I say you are a girl. Please decide for us. Enclosed find stamp for reply. P.S. Do you play tennis?"

Very little about Nellie's personal life appeared in her stories, even when she was writing lighthearted pieces. Elizabeth Cochrane had the same problems of balancing a career and a personal life that women with jobs face today, but she had no one else's experiences to help her decide how to handle them.

Her pioneering efforts in journalism kept her from participating in many of the normal activities of a young woman in the nineteenth century. Career women with whom she might have had something in common were either radical feminists with whom she could not agree, or professional rivals who could not be trusted. Just as her publisher considered all other newspaper publishers to be competitors, Nellie had to suspect all other newspaperwomen of being out to "scoop" her, or steal her ideas. In her off-duty hours, she usually spent time with her mother.

Mrs. Cochran came to New York soon after the Blackwell's Island episode, and kept house for Nellie in an uptown flat. A number of escorts took them both to the theater and to parties, but most of Nellie's life revolved around her work.

She first revealed her sense of humor to her reading public in an article that appeared on December 18, 1887—a three-column story about her attempt to learn ballet. Not only was ballet harder than she had expected, she told her readers, but the ballet skirts were *very* short. Nellie later decided that showing her legs was not all that terrible. To get another story, she appeared on stage in a chorus line.

Her fellow reporters knew about the performance in advance, and filled the theater to see "Nellie Bly on the Stage." Her article had the subtitle

NELLIE BLY ON THE STAGE.

SHE WEARS A SCANT COSTUME AND MARCHES WITH THE AMAZONS.

It Isn't Very Hard to Get Such a Job—The Girls Earn $5 a Week—Tights that Did Not Fit—Dressing in a Crowded Room—How She Behaved on the Stage—A Bad Beginning.

I MADE my début as a chorus girl or stage Amazon last week. It was my first appearance on any stage and came about through reading among THE WORLD advertisements one that called for 100 girls for a spectacular pantomime, so I found myself one afternoon at the stage door of the Academy of Music. There were but two men there. I looked at them and they looked at me, and as nobody made any movement to speak, I asked:

"Where do I go in answer to the advertisement?"

The opening paragraphs of Nellie's column about her adventure as a "stage Amazon," or chorus girl.

"She Wears a Scant Costume and Marches with the Amazons," and a sketch showed her holding her shield and spear.

This story started when Nellie saw an advertisement in the *World* for a hundred showgirls for "a spectacular pantomime." At the Academy of Music, she was hired without an audition and told to come back at seven. There was no rehearsal. Her instructions were to "walk between girls who know the routine and they will tell you what to do."

"My garments were too big," Nellie told her readers, "my ballet slippers four sizes too long.... My white wig was so small my own dark hair showed underneath it. The helmet was so large it kept slipping back on my head. I was a sad sight!"

"You started on the wrong foot," the girl next to her hissed.

"You've got your shield on the wrong arm," said the Amazon on her other side.

"Face about!" came the order from the stage manager.

Nellie faced left. Everyone else turned right. She hurriedly corrected her position, but things continued to get worse. "The other girls had marched to the side of the stage and divided," she wrote. "I was left standing in the center of the stage, all alone. With more haste than grace, I ran after them, thankful to get away from it all."

Nellie's lighthearted articles included a number of interviews. She talked with Buffalo Bill backstage at his Wild West Show, and with eight women who had occupied the White House. One, Mrs. Grover Cleveland, was married to the current president. Five were widows of past presidents. The other two, Mrs. Harriet Johnson, the niece of President James Buchanan, and Mrs. John McElroy, the sister of President Chester A. Arthur, had served as hostesses for unmarried presidents.

Nellie traveled around the country to meet and talk with these women, but she found a more interesting interview in New York City. It was with Belva Lockwood, a lawyer who was running for president in 1888 as an independent candidate. She was probably the first women's rights activist Nellie Bly ever talked with at length.

"Do you truly expect to be elected president?" Nellie asked her.

"Certainly," said Mrs. Lockwood, who was gray-haired and self-assured and wore black-rimmed eyeglasses.

"Have you any newspapers backing you?" Nellie asked.

"No," Mrs. Lockwood told her. "There is nothing to make it worth their while yet."

"Do all women support you?"

"Thinking women and working women do. Society women never go outside of society. The very poor, the masses, are no better. One is the doll, the other the slave."

At that time, women did not have the right to vote. Mrs. Lockwood had to overcome many obstacles in order to become a lawyer in a profession few women had been allowed to enter. When Nellie asked her what she thought of President Cleveland's chances for re-election, she replied, "Why, he's not the candidate. Mrs. Cleveland is."

Nellie never became an activist for women's rights, but she did write a flattering, positive article about Mrs. Lockwood. "She is a womanly woman," she wrote. "What greater praise can one give her? She is firm and intelligent without being manly, and gentle and womanly without being frivolous. She is the beau ideal of a woman with a brain."

The famous blizzard of March 1888 brought romance into Nellie Bly's life, although at first it was just another amusing anecdote to tell her readers. One morning during the worst of the storm, she slipped on the icy sidewalk and went flying. Nellie cried, "Good-by, perpendicular!" as her feet went out from under her. She ended up sprawled on the pavement. A handsome, violet-eyed stranger appeared, helped her up, brushed her off, and went on his way. Later, she learned that he was James Metcalfe, the editor of a humorous weekly magazine called *Life*.

After that unusual first meeting, Metcalfe frequently escorted Nellie and her mother to shows and parties. Yet even with such a dashing companion, Nellie was getting bored. She was ready for a new challenge, and she knew just what it was going to be.

One of the legends in Nellie's family concerned her mother's uncle, Thomas Kennedy. He had made a trip around the world that had taken three years. More recently, in 1872, Jules Verne had published an adventure novel, *Around the World in Eighty Days*. These two globe-trotting stories had given Nellie an idea. She would travel around the world and beat the record set by Verne's imaginary character, Phileas Fogg. Think of the publicity for the *World*! thought Nellie. Think of the adventures she could have! She went to Joseph Pulitzer, enthusiastic about the project.

But Joseph Pulitzer wasn't so sure it would work. This stunt of Nellie's was bigger than anything she had tried before. A trip around the world could be dangerous, too, especially for a woman alone. She reminded him she had gone to Mexico and returned unharmed. She also mentioned all the risks she had taken on stories for his newspaper.

Pulitzer said he would think about it, and he did—for almost a year. He consulted with his business manager, G. W. Turner, with John Cockerill, who was now editor-in-chief, and with the new managing editor, the same Julius Chambers who had taken a reporting assignment at the mental hospital. Finally they decided to go ahead, but to send a man, a reporter named John Jennings, instead of Nellie Bly.

"If you do," Nellie told Mr. Pulitzer, "I'll leave at the same time and race against him." Nellie threatened to quit, finance her own trip, and challenge the reporter the *World* sent out.

Reluctantly, and with many reservations, Pulitzer gave her his approval. Could she be ready to leave in three days? he asked. Now that he was committed, he didn't want any other newspaper sending a reporter on a trip around the world before Nellie Bly.

Chapter/Eight

Around the World

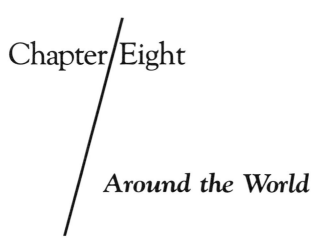

Although Nellie had been told that she would have three days to get ready, she actually had four, and she needed every minute. She bought a twenty-four-hour watch, so that she would know every second whether she was on schedule or not. She kept that in a pocket, set on New York time. On her wrist she wore a watch to be set to the local times of the places she would pass through during her trip.

In this era before backpacks and strong, light-weight fabrics, Nellie had a hard time finding what she wanted to use for luggage. Finally she chose a small suitcase, or gripsack, of crocodile skin and a second tweed bag that she could hang over her shoulder.

When it came time to fill them, her first stop

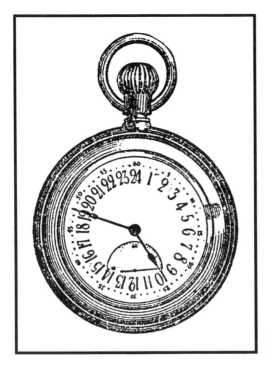

A drawing of Nellie's twenty-four-hour watch.

was Ghormley's, a dressmaking establishment on East Nineteenth Street. Nellie made Mr. William Ghormley swear to keep her trip a secret, and offered him a deal. If he could finish the garments she needed in time, she would list his products in her account of her trip.

Because of her promise to Mr. Ghormley, and because she knew her readers would be interested, Nellie recorded every item she packed. Into those two small bags went flannel underwear, handkerchiefs, a dressing gown, slippers, two of the three "ghillie" caps (also known as deerstalkers) she had found at Ghormley's, three veils, a tennis blazer, needles and thread, toilet articles, an inkstand, pens and pencils, copy paper, a flask and drinking cup, and a jar of cold cream. She packed two silk blouses that could be worn with the skirt of her one dress, a sturdy blue plaid broadcloth. She had a gossamer silk raincoat that she planned to carry over one arm, and she would wear the coat that was to become her trademark—a fashionable Scotch plaid ulster (overcoat) with a little cape. Nellie also carried a passport, visas, tickets, reservations, two hundred pounds in English money, and five hundred dollars in American gold and paper money. These valuables went inside in a small chamois purse she could sling around her neck.

While Nellie packed, the *World* made travel arrangements. She would leave on Thursday, November 14, 1889, on the steamer *Augusta Victoria*, which was scheduled to sail from Jersey City, New Jersey, at 9:30 A.M. If all went well, Nellie would be back in the *World* offices in New York seventy-five days later, on January 27, 1890.

The *Augusta Victoria* left ten minutes and six seconds later than scheduled, and a timekeeper from the New York Athletic Club kept the official record. Nellie's mother was there to see her off, peering through her spectacles and the mist for a

last glimpse of her remarkable daughter. Julius Chambers came to write the report that would appear in the same day's *Evening World*. Only one or two others even knew Nellie was leaving, because the *World* wanted the entire stunt kept secret until Chambers's story appeared.

"Around the World" the headline read, and next to that column a map of Nellie's journey stretched across the page. There was a sketch, too, of Nellie aboard the ship, gripsack in hand.

"The *World* today undertakes the task of turning a dream into a reality," the article began. She set forth, it said, "chic and pert in her double-peaked cap of light drag, showing not a wince of fear or trepidation."

The biggest problem with coverage of Nellie Bly's trip around the world was communication. It seems impossible now, when live satellite reports can be beamed anywhere in seconds, but in 1889 it took seventeen days for Nellie's first stories to make their way back to the *World* from London. Often, the *World* staff in New York had no idea where their star reporter was. There were times, too, when false reports reached them, but the bits and pieces the *World* did receive from Nellie kept its readers eager for more.

To fill the time between reports, the *World*

Nellie Bly, dressed for her around-the-world trip. She is wearing the plaid ulster coat that later became her trademark.

supplied a Nellie Bly Board Game, printed on a two-page fold-out. A Nellie Bly Guessing Game offered $250 and a trip to Europe to the *World* reader who came the closest to guessing the exact time of her return to her starting point in Jersey City. The paper also answered questions about Nellie for her fans. Was she really a man? some readers still asked. No, the *World* replied. She was a quiet and reserved brunette who liked horseback riding and could ride a tricycle. She did not chew gum, or have any other unladylike habits.

Meanwhile, Nellie traveled aboard the *Augusta Victoria*, with time to rest and plan ahead. There was nothing she could do to make it go any faster, and it would not arrive in London for a week. At first the seas were rough and Nellie was seasick, but she soon recovered. By the second day she had her sea legs and was writing stories about her fellow passengers.

When the *Augusta Victoria* docked at Southampton, England, at 2:00 A.M. on November 22, Nellie traveled at once to London. She arrived there at 5:00 A.M. and sent a cable back to New York in code. It said, "I'm all right—letter follows." Then she added that she had made a slight change in the schedule.

Nellie had discovered that by going 180 miles

A FREE TRIP TO EUROPE!

(Including first-class transatlantic passages, railroad fares and hotel bills)

TO THE PERSON WHO FIRST MAKES

THE NEAREST GUESS

AS TO THE

EXACT TIME OF NELLIE BLY'S TOUR.

NEXT SUNDAY'S WORLD

WILL PRINT A

NELLIE BLY BLANK BALLOT.

Upon this blank ballot all guesses must be made, the ballots being cut out and mailed to THE SUNDAY WORLD. Guesses not made on THE WORLD blanks cannot compete. Only one guess can be made on a single blank, but any reader of THE SUNDAY WORLD can send in as many guesses as he or she pleases, by procuring extra blanks from extra copies of THE SUNDAY WORLD. Full particulars Sunday. There will be an extraordinary demand for these blank ballots, and you should not fail to

Order Next SUNDAY'S WORLD at Once.

The World *kept the story of Nellie's journey in the news partly by sponsoring this contest.*

out of her way, she could visit Jules Verne and his wife at their estate in Amiens, France. This side trip was one of the highlights of the journey for Nellie, but to make it she took a terrible risk of missing her travel connections.

Verne had brilliant black eyes, she reported, and a white beard, and walked with a slight limp. He met her at the station with a startled, "Why, she is a mere baby!"

At Verne's house, Nellie asked if she might see the desk where he wrote his novels. "I had expected to see a hand-carved desk filled with trinkets, but I saw only a plain, flat-topped one. It was in a small room, modest and bare, with a single latticed window." In the hall was a map of the world, showing Phileas Fogg's journey.

"If you do it in seventy-nine days," Jules Verne told her, "I shall applaud with both hands. But seventy-five days—mon Dieu—that would be a miracle!"

Nellie sent back another cable when she had mailed in her interview with Verne: "To all kind friends in America, good-by for the present. It took sharp work to catch the Brindisi mail train, but I got it."

The English government operated a train through France and Italy to meet the Peninsular and

Oriental Line steamers and gain five days in the delivery of mail from India and Australia. It had one passenger coach, with one attendant—porter, guard, steward, cook, and brakeman all in one. In Brindisi, Italy, Nellie boarded the steamer *Victoria*, bound for Colombo, Ceylon, in the Indian Ocean. It left at 2:00 A.M. on November 25, and arrived in Ceylon on December 8.

Newspapers all over the world were reporting on Nellie Bly's incredible journey. Her fellow passengers were interested, too, and she received several proposals of marriage on the way. Nellie had other, more immediate concerns. Her ship, the Peninsular and Oriental Line steamer, arrived two days behind schedule. Then her next ship, the *Oriental*, delayed its departure until December 10 to wait for the passengers from another vessel. Nellie sent cables and shopped, since there was little else she could do. Singapore was two thousand miles away, and there was no other way to get there.

Nellie experimented during the delays with different local methods of travel. By the end of her journey she could say that she had been transported by train and ship, mule and bullock cart, catamaran and sampan, and "half a dozen other conveyances peculiar to Eastern countries."

In Singapore, there was another delay, and it

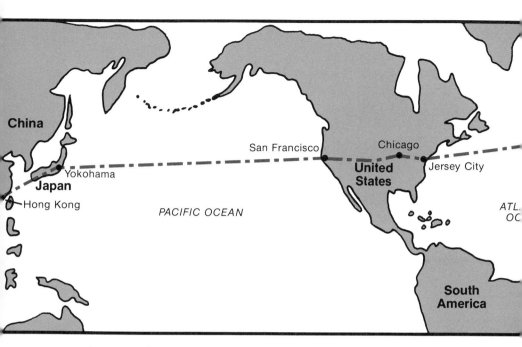

The route of Nellie's trip around the world.

was already December 18. While she waited, Nellie took a side trip into China, where she bought a macaque, a short-tailed monkey. By the time the *Oriental* set sail for Hong Kong, Nellie's spirits were high. They lifted even higher when she spotted her next vessel, the White Star steamship *Oceanic*, waiting in port to take her back to America for the last leg of her journey. At the offices of the Occidental and Oriental Steamship Company, though, she received some surprising news.

"You're going to be beaten," she was told.

"I think not," Nellie replied, surprised by such

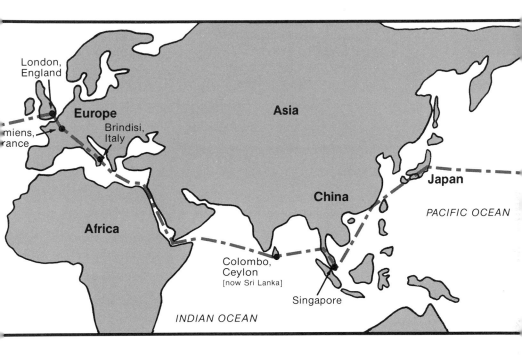

a statement. "I have made up my delay."

"You are going to lose it," the officer insisted.

"I don't understand you," Nellie said. "I'm on time. It's only December twenty-second."

"But the other woman, she came in on the *Oceanic* and has already started south. You passed her halfway up from Singapore. She's a good five days ahead of you."

This was how Nellie first heard of her competition. They told her the other woman had been sent by the *World*, but that was not true. Her name was Elizabeth Bisland, and she was literary editor of

Cosmopolitan magazine. She had been sent to race the *World* reporter by traveling in the opposite direction. She had left New York in the evening of the same day Nellie sailed, heading west by train. She had arrived in Japan the same day Nellie reached Ceylon, and had left Hong Kong on December 18, the day Nellie arrived in Singapore.

Despite the frustrating delays and moments of despair, Nellie was more determined than ever to hurry now that she knew she had competition. She was also determined to bring her monkey home with her.

On her way to her cabin on the *Oceanic,* Nellie met the stewardess. "I have a monkey," Nellie started to tell her.

"We have met," the stewardess said. Her arm was covered with monkey bites and scratches.

Fortunately, the stewardess shared the attitude of the rest of the crew—a desire to travel even faster going to San Francisco with Nellie than they had coming out with Elizabeth Bisland. That had been a record-breaking trip—seventeen days to Japan—but in the engine room they wrote this rhyme on the wall: "For Nellie Bly / We'll do or die. January 20, 1890." January 20 was her deadline for reaching San Francisco if she were to be back in New Jersey on schedule.

"Don't you fret," the chief engineer teased her. "If they fire you, I'll marry you."

The *Oceanic* left Hong Kong on December 28, and all went well as far as Yokohama, Japan. Then, soon after the *Oceanic* left that port on January 7, 1890, it encountered a monsoon, a storm with strong winds and heavy rains.

"It's the monkey's fault," a superstitious sailor told Nellie. "Monkeys are bad luck on a ship. The storm won't die down until he's thrown overboard."

Nellie wasn't about to part with her pet. She went to the captain. "I understand ministers, too, are Jonahs [bad luck]," she said. "There are two ministers on this ship. If you throw them overboard, I'll let you throw my monkey as well."

She might have tried to make jokes, but she was worried. The longer the storm raged around them, the longer it would take to reach San Francisco. When the skies finally cleared, they sped on across the Pacific Ocean. The *Oceanic* arrived in San Francisco Bay less than twenty-four hours behind Nellie's schedule for her round-the-world trip.

A huge crowd had gathered to meet her in San Francisco, even though it was only 7:30 in the morning. A band played "Home Sweet Home" and "Nelly Bly" and some new songs that had been written about Nellie while she was away. A parade marched her to the train station, where a special car waited. Breakfast was waiting, too, along with news of more difficulties ahead. The railroad officials told her that she could not follow her original route because blizzards were raging across the country. In fact, the *World* reporters who were coming to meet her in San Francisco had been stranded aboard another train somewhere in the mountains. The interest in Nellie's trip had grown so much, though, that the railroads had made special arrangements for her. At 9:00 A.M. the engine pulled out of San Francisco, headed east via a brand new route. Nellie's special train followed Southern Pacific tracks to Mohave, took the Atlantic and Pacific and the Atcheson, Topeka, and Santa Fe lines to Kansas City, and then sped on to Chicago.

John Jennings, the reporter Pulitzer had wanted to send around the world instead of Nellie, met her train two hours into the journey. He had hiked eight hours on snowshoes from the snowbound train to catch up with her.

At every coaling stop, crowds gathered to see Nellie Bly. In Chicago, where she changed trains and had a two-hour layover, she was taken to breakfast at the Chicago Press Club. Nellie was the first woman reporter they had ever allowed in the door. At

This cartoon from the World showed Nellie's place as first among explorers who had circled the globe.

10:41 A.M. she was on her way again on the Chicago Limited Express.

In Pittsburg, a huge crowd came to the station to greet Nellie. The Pittsburg Order of Elks elected her an honorary member. In Philadelphia she changed trains for the last time, and was joined by James Metcalfe, Julius Chambers, and her mother.

Finally, at 3:51 P.M. on January 25, Nellie Bly's train reached Jersey City. Officially, the trip lasted seventy-two days, six hours, and eleven minutes—a record which would remain unbroken until 1929 when the *Graf Zeppelin*, an airship, circled the globe

FATHER TIME OUTDONE !

Even Imagination's Record Pales Before the Performance of " The World's " Globe-Circler.

HER TIME : 72 DAYS, 6 HRS., 11 MIN.. -- SEC.

Thousands Cheer Themselves Hoarse at Nellie Bly's Arrival.

WELCOME. SALUTES IN NEW YORK AND BROOKLYN.

The Whole Country Aglow with Intense Enthusiasm.

NELLIE BLY TELLS HER STORY.

The World's announcement of Nellie's successful return.

in twenty days, four hours, and fourteen minutes. Elizabeth Bisland was still several days away from New York and the completion of her trip around the world.

Jersey City's mayor welcomed Nellie and declared that "the American girl can no longer be misunderstood. She will be recognized as pushing, determined, independent, able to take care of herself wherever she may go."

"I feel like a successful presidential candidate," Nellie told the crowd. She was eager, however, to go on to New York City. For her, the 24,899-mile trip was not over; it would end only when she was back at the *World*.

Ten guns boomed to welcome her home, and at 4:30 P.M. she entered her own office, triumphant and smiling. She wasn't allowed to stay long, not even to write a story. The nearby Astor House had a champagne reception in her honor. Nellie Bly was, for the moment, the most famous person in America.

Chapter/Nine

I May Say All I Please

It didn't take long for Nellie to begin writing about her journey. In addition to her stories for the *World*, she wrote *Nellie Bly's Book: Around the World in 72 Days*. Her picture appeared everywhere in advertisements for Pears Soap—though her own complexion was now tanned an unfashionable brown—and other products. She took advantage of her fame to earn more money than she had ever been able to before—about $25,000 in 1890. At that time it was enough to build a house for herself and her mother and still have a large sum left to save for other needs.

The monkey that Nellie brought home with her proved a disappointment as a house pet. It broke every dish in her apartment during the few days it

lived there. Nellie eventually donated the little crea-
ture to Central Park Zoo.

Nellie soon accepted a contract to tour the
country, lecturing about her adventures abroad. She
wore her famous traveling costume from Ghormley's and told her listeners that no place in the world
was as good as America. They, in turn, were de-
lighted to hear that the Italian trains were always
late, and that the British crew members on the *Victoria* were irresponsible and rude.

In her lectures, she described her adventures
to the eager crowds. She told one story about her
voyage to Singapore. During the trip, she had had
trouble sleeping, and having her sleep disturbed, she
said, "makes me as ill-natured as a bad dinner
makes a man." A nurse and two children were staying in the cabin next to her. Every morning the
father, who had a cabin on the other side of the
ship, came to the door of their cabin and shouted
good morning at them. The children would shout
back. Then the father would bellow, "What does
Baby say to Mamma?" "Mamma!" one of the children would shout. "What does Baby say to Papa?"
"Papa!" "What does the moo-moo cow say?" And
so it went.

"If it had been once, or twice even," Nellie said,
"I might have endured it with civilized forbearance,

but after it had been repeated...every morning for six long weary mornings, my temper gave way, and when he said, 'Tell Papa what the moo-moo cow says?' I shouted frantically: 'For heaven's sake, Baby, tell Papa what the moo-moo cow says, and let me go to sleep!'"

Nellie had not stayed long enough in any port to get to know its people, but that did not stop her from making judgments about them with the same crisp descriptions she used in her interviews. As she did in Mexico, she tended to make generalizations about the conditions she saw without understanding the culture that produced them.

While Nellie Bly toured America, a series of articles was published in *Cosmopolitan* under the title "A Flying Trip Around the World." Elizabeth Bisland had arrived in New York four days after Nellie's triumphant return, to be met quietly at the dock by a few friends. Bisland did not beat Nellie Bly, but she did beat the record set by Jules Verne's character. She completed her trip in seventy-six days, and went on to achieve modest success as a foreign correspondent, biographer, and novelist. She and Nellie never met.

In the fall of 1893, Nellie signed a contract which provided for one leading newspaper in each community to carry her weekly stories. In New

Nellie's Sunday column was read by people across the country.

York it was the *Sunday World.* "Nellie Bly's Column" gave her freedom from any one editor's control, although she had an office in the World building. She could travel anywhere in search of stories. As she wrote in the first column, "this is all my own...I may say all I please and what I please." Above each column was a sketch of Nellie Bly. The sketches changed, depending on the story she was writing.

Nellie's stories had lost none of their impact. She wrote an article in praise of the Salvation Army, which brought in huge amounts of money for its cause. A less serious story described society women who were haunting pool rooms and betting on races. Undercover investigations revealed a mind-reader as a fraud and addressed serious social issues, too.

From 1893 until 1898, America was in an economic depression. Many radical proposals were made to correct the situation, including anarchy, or removing government authority altogether. For one of her first columns, Nellie decided to interview the woman known as the "queen of the anarchists" in her prison cell.

Emma Goldman was in jail on a charge of causing riots when Nellie interviewed her in September 1893. As she had when she interviewed Belva Lockwood, Nellie reported the interview almost word for word, allowing Goldman to express her point of view. Putting aside her own political opinions, Nellie tried to be as fair and objective as possible in this kind of article.

"If you do away with money and employers," Nellie asked, "who will work upon your railroads?"

"Those who like that kind of work. Everyone should do that which he likes best, not a thing that he is compelled to do to earn his daily bread."

"What would you do with the lazy ones who would not work?" Nellie asked.

Emma Goldman shortly before she was put in prison.

"No one is lazy," Emma said. "They grow hopeless from the misery of their existence and give up. Under our order of things, every man would do the work he liked best and would have as much as his neighbor, so could not be unhappy or discouraged."

Later Nellie asked Emma why she didn't believe in marriage. "I believe in the marriage of affection," Emma answered.

"What about children?" Nellie asked. She pointed out that if men and women just lived together, "Men would desert; women and children would be left uncared for and destitute."

"On the contrary," Emma argued. "Men would never desert. If a couple decided to separate, there would be public homes and schools for the children. Mothers who would rather do something other than care for children could put them in schools, where they would be cared for by women who preferred taking care of children to anything else in life. In this way, we would never have diseased or disabled children from careless and incompetent mothers."

Emma Goldman's theories were very radical for 1893, but Nellie, listening, must have thought of herself. She had not followed the traditional route of marriage or motherhood. In fact, now that she was in her mid-twenties, many people thought of her as an "old maid" who would never marry or have children.

In the spring of 1895, Nellie went west to write about farmers in Nebraska and South Dakota whose farmland had been ruined by a severe drought. The trip had two positive results: food and medical aid were sent from New York, and Nellie met a seventy-two-year-old hardware manufacturer named Robert L. Seaman on a train traveling west. It was a meeting that would change her life.

"Her marriage," the *World* reported, "like most of the other important events in Nellie Bly's life, was out of the ordinary. She met her husband on the train, on the way to Chicago, only a few days before she became a bride." Although they had just met, Robert Seaman knew about Nellie through her newspaper writing.

Robert Seaman, who was senior director of the Merchants' Exchange National Bank of New York and president of the Iron Clad Manufacturing Company, had gone to Chicago to attend a business convention. He and Nellie were married soon after her return to New York, in the Church of the Epiphany, on April 5, 1895. Nellie was just a month short of her twenty-eighth birthday.

Some people accused Nellie of being a "gold

digger," because her new husband was forty-four years older than she and because he was a millionaire five times over. "They are wrong," Nellie said, but she did not feel the need to justify herself. Nellie had always considered her personal life to be a private matter. When she married, she did not tell her readers anything about her plans. All they knew came from an article in the *World*. "Miss Bly," it reported, "will become the mistress of a metropolitan residence, a magnificent country seat, a whole stableful of horses, and nearly everything the good fairy of the story books always pictures. Few young women have had more worldly experience than Miss Bly and few are more capable of enjoying the pleasures of a millionaire's existence."

The marriage of two people accustomed to independence required making adjustments. Nellie was not in the habit of telling anyone where she was going. Headstrong, she resented her new husband's questions. Jealous, he hired a private detective to follow her. When Nellie realized she was being tailed, she had the detective arrested. Her husband bailed him out, and the next day the charges against him were dismissed. Nellie would later write that "what passes for love is generally selfishness. Real love is wholly unselfish. It is something the angels in Heaven might envy."

An advertisement promoting Nellie's manufacturing company.

Soon, the newlyweds worked out their differences and began to travel. Seaman had many friends and business acquaintances in Europe. In November 1897, on a visit to Wiesbaden, Germany, Nellie met Bertha Krupp, a woman who "was doing great things in a business left her by her people." Her example inspired Nellie, and when they returned home, Robert Seaman gave his wife her own business to run.

The Iron Clad Manufacturing Company factory in Brooklyn, New York, made milk cans, soda fountains, and range boilers. Nellie had seen steel milk cans in Europe and set out to design her own model. Her first experiment leaked. The second and third versions also had problems, but at last she developed a successful product, which she patented.

Several years passed during which Nellie dabbled in business, enjoyed her four-story brownstone mansion in Manhattan and three-hundred-acre farm in New York State's Greene County, and did charity work. Then, on March 11, 1904, Robert Seaman died of a heart attack.

Nellie had no children, and since her marriage she had not worked as a journalist. Now, with her husband suddenly gone, she needed an outlet for her energy. She focused her attention on the factory he had given her.

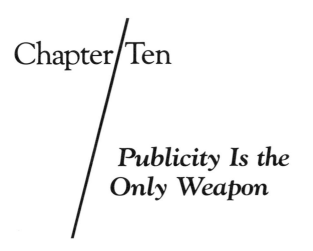

Chapter/Ten

Publicity Is the Only Weapon

In five years Nellie Seaman had founded the American Steel Barrel Company and built it into the largest factory of its kind in the country. She had changed to modern methods, built a new factory across the street from the Iron Clad plant, raised wages, and put a large club room and dining room in the Iron Clad building for the employees of both companies.

During those same years, Nellie discovered prejudice against women in the business world. "They tolerate us women now down in the clerical classes," she wrote, "but when we try for anything more, why we get ahead only so far as we can fight our way against obstacles from which a business-man...is...free."

In 1905, Nellie discovered that the Dairymen's Manufacturing Company was making and selling milk cans using her patented design. She took legal action, but just before she was to travel north to Herkimer County to testify in court, she received two phone calls. The first attempted to bribe her. The second was a threat.

Nellie reported them and went through with her testimony. "Until business men learn that the woman in business is entitled to the same fairness that exists between men, there will be no place in business for women," she wrote. Meanwhile, she intended "to fight the infinitely numerous crooked games tried upon us."

At the time of the Herkimer County trial, Nellie had already been in and out of other courtrooms for months. One of her business problems was a fire, which destroyed a four-story frame building containing the milling department of the Iron Clad Manufacturing Company. Also, an audit revealed that two of her employees had been forging her name to checks. When creditors asked the court to declare her company bankrupt, the factory was closed. Now Nellie had no way to earn the money to pay her bills. Two years of court battles followed.

During bankruptcy proceedings, Nellie traveled to Albany to see Governor John Alden Dix of New

York. "I want to find out if the State of New York will allow a woman engaged in a legitimate business to be robbed as I have been robbed," she said. Apparently, it would.

Finally, Nellie turned to the newspapers. "Publicity is the only weapon left," she declared. While articles in the New York *Times* did say that she had been cheated by the forgers, an editorial blamed her problems on her "incomplete business training." The article ended by saying, "her belief that every man's hand is against her simply because she is a woman in business can be understood and even excused, but fortunately it is not true. Further proclamation of it, now that the court has spoken, might lead to the suspicion that what the woman in business wants is not justice, or such justice as would be accorded a man, but consideration of her femininity—which would be both unreasonable and impracticable."

Nellie still did not give up. She wrote an article for a weekly magazine, *Fair Play*, titled "How I was Robbed of Two Million Dollars." But on the same day copies arrived at newsstands, January 18, 1912, they were removed. Claiming that the article "contained the possibility of libel," the newsstands refused to sell it.

In early March, Nellie was charged with

contempt of court for failing to answer questions
from the referee in the bankruptcy proceedings. She
defended herself by pleading "a physical and mental
strain for something like two years that would have
broken down many a strong man." On March 26,
though, she was fined six hundred dollars and given
until March 30 to pay. A second contempt of court
charge followed when Nellie could not produce her
former auditor.

The court battle dragged on into 1914, when
Nellie had to pay $50,000 and withdraw all claims
against Iron Clad Manufacturing. She still faced contempt charges, and expected to be sued by her lawyer, whose bill she had refused to pay when he
overcharged her. Badly in need of rest, she boarded
a ship bound for Europe, intending to have a short
visit with friends in Austria and plan her next move.
Instead, she was away for nearly five years.

She was delayed by the outbreak of World
War I. At first everyone thought the war would be
over in a few weeks. Nellie stayed in Vienna and
began to send back news stories. Her business problems at home seemed to be resolving themselves,
and in Austria, life was pleasant. Nellie was enjoying
the company of an old friend, Oscar Bondy, and she
saw no reason to rush back to America.

Nellie stayed on and on, lulled into a false sense

Nellie Bly in her later years.

of security by her well-to-do Viennese friends. But in April 1917, America entered the war—on the Allied side with France and Great Britain—against Austria and the other Central Powers. Suddenly Nellie was the enemy. She was now forbidden to leave Vienna, for fear she would carry back information about conditions there.

The winter of 1917-1918 was worse than the one before. When starvation threatened and food rationing was enforced, strikes and riots erupted on the streets. Yet another terrible winter was approaching when the war ended in November 1918. Vienna was freezing, and there was no fuel. By mid-January 1919, there were demonstrations and violence, but by then Nellie had finally headed home.

Chapter/Eleven

Back to Work

The newspaper world had not forgotten Nellie Bly. When she arrived in New York, the press was there to greet her. She was "as vivacious as the indefatigable, fearless investigator of years ago," said the Brooklyn *Eagle*. Wearing silks and furs, she impressed the reporter with her "striking personality." The accounts were somewhat vague about why she had been in Europe. She had arrived from France, one reported, where she had been doing "war work."

In a letter to Erasmus Wilson, a reporter for the *Dispatch*, Nellie wrote, "I returned after all these years to find...I have exactly $3.65 and a trunk full of Paris evening dresses."

On March 4, 1919, Nellie was back in court in

Brooklyn. In 1915, while she was in Europe, she had been accused of trying to hide her company's books. Though the case had been dismissed, the years of court battles and her long absence had weakened Nellie's enthusiasm for a business career. While she was in Austria, her brother Albert had mismanaged the family business. Nellie quarreled with her mother over that, and instead of moving in with her, took rooms in the Hotel McAlpin. She was not poor, but she needed a job.

Newspaper work was Nellie Bly's goal at eighteen. At fifty-two it was still her best means of earning a living. Arthur Brisbane had been managing editor of the *Sunday World* when Nellie left the newspaper to get married. Now he was editor of the New York *Evening Journal*. Soon after her return from Europe, he proposed that she come to work for him. He offered her a job as a columnist and told her that she could use her regular column to further the cause of abandoned children. Nellie Bly, reformer and reporter, went back to work.

Her fame and fortune had faded, as had her youth and health. Nellie had gained so much weight that it was hard to recognize her as the young woman who had traveled around the world. At the *Journal* she had her own office, and there she seemed to hide from her fellow reporters. She came

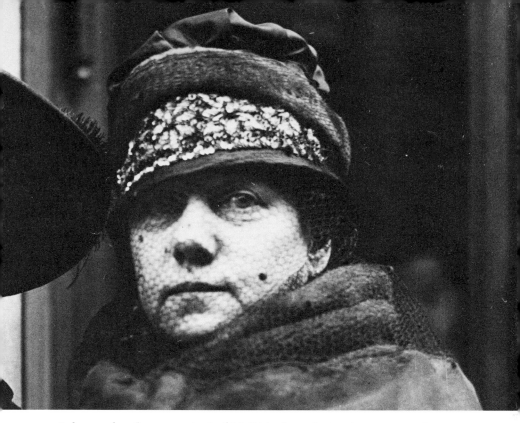

A hat and veil were typical of Nellie's dress during her years at the Journal.

in every day, but her face was hidden by large hats with veils covered with chenille dots.

A campaign to save homeless children took up much of Nellie's time. As early as 1880, 100,000 children lived on the streets of New York City. Now street urchins were everywhere, sleeping in doorways, in ash cans, under stairs, in boxes, and in barrels. Some had run away from homes where they had been mistreated. Others had been thrown out by uncaring parents. To eat, they scrounged in the garbage outside of grocery stores and restaurants.

Several societies helped such children—the

New York Society for the Prevention of Cruelty to Children, the Children's Aid Society, and the Children's Relief Society—but more help was needed. Nellie convinced millionaire Edwin Gould to form the Gould Foundation to help homeless children. She also used her column to find homes for babies whose parents could not afford to keep them.

On December 9, a man handed a baby boy to a Grand Central Station security guard named Harry Loise. Then he disappeared. A note in the child's clothes said: "For the Love of Mike, Somebody, take this kid. He is one too much for the family. Give him to Nellie Bly of the New York Journal. He is 7 months old and as healthy as they make 'em. Can't afford him on the price of milk they are charging today. There are others I am trying to support."

The baby was taken to Bellevue Hospital, and Nellie was notified. Because of the personal appeal to her in the note, she decided to adopt the child herself. The legal arrangements were soon completed. By December 16, Nellie had hired a nurse and was ready to sign the final papers. At the last moment, however, Mrs. August Wentz came forward and claimed that the baby was her son, who had been kidnapped in July. The hospital let Mrs. Wentz take the little boy home, although she had no proof the child was hers.

Understandably, Nellie was upset. She announced that she would keep the identity of the real mother secret if the mother would contact her. All the papers ran the story, and as Nellie was leaving her hotel on the morning of December 17, she was approached by Harry Loise and a hysterical young woman. She turned out to be the baby's mother, a widow named Lena Lisa.

Mrs. Lisa was a flower arranger, a job that did not pay enough for her to hire someone to care for her three small children. Since she had not been able to afford to take a day off to bring the baby to Nellie herself, she asked a friend to do it for her. He had not known where to find the newspaper reporter, so he had written the note and left the baby, whose name was Enrico, with Loise. After she heard this story, Nellie decided to recover the baby from Mrs. Wentz, give it back to Mrs. Lisa, and then help her get a better job.

"It's a pack of lies," Mrs. Wentz protested. "Miss Bly is all mistaken. This baby is mine, and it's here to stay."

On December 18, though, Nellie took Mrs. Lisa and her three-year-old son, William, to the Wentz home. Little Enrico recognized his mother and brother, making his identity clear. After a good deal of crying, everyone then went to children's

court, and the baby was returned to Mrs. Lisa.

Nellie lost her chance to become Enrico Lisa's mother, but the publicity had two immediate results. Editorials began to call for fingerprinting of newborn babies, so that they could be accurately identified. Also, Mrs. Ida Magerhaus contacted Nellie to ask if she would adopt her daughter, Frances, who had been born July 15, 1919.

Nellie had become attached to the idea of motherhood, and in the days after Mrs. Lisa took back her child, she made an impulsive decision. She would adopt the Magerhaus baby. On December 31, the child legally became Elizabeth Seaman, and Nellie took her back to the McAlpin.

Nellie soon realized that she had made a mistake. She could not take care of the child properly and also perform well at work. Still, she had to keep her job in order to afford the rooms at the McAlpin. Her only solution was to find better parents for the child. On January 9, Nellie appeared in surrogate's court with Mr. and Mrs. Francois de Sasso and gave up her claim to the baby in their favor.

This was not an easy decision for Nellie to make, and the strain might have affected her coverage of her next assignment for the *Journal*. She was sent to interview a murderer who was awaiting execution in Sing Sing prison. Nellie used this

Nellie Bly (right) *posed with Mrs. Lena Lisa and two of her children shortly after Nellie returned Mrs. Lisa's baby.*

opportunity to make a plea for abolishing capital punishment. In the process, she also made another bit of history. On January 29, 1920, she became the first woman in twenty-nine years to witness an execution in New York State. "Horrible! Horrible! Horrible!" she began her article, but her crusade against the death penalty was not a success.

In 1921, Nellie's mother died. She had continued to live in the house Nellie built for her, along with Nellie's brother Albert. Since Nellie had cut ties with both of them, Mrs. Cochran left everything she owned to Albert. In October, Albert held an auction to sell the contents of the house.

Nellie was a patient in St. Mark's hospital when she heard about the auction. She was so furious that she ordered a car and persuaded a nurse to take her there in a wheelchair. She had the police arrest Albert on a charge of grand larceny, claiming he had already sold thousands of dollars worth of furniture and antiques that rightfully belonged to her. Nellie's health was failing rapidly, and the family feud added to the strains on her. When she left the hospital, she was far from well. The following January, while she was covering a story for the *Journal*, she caught pneumonia.

Nellie Bly died on January 27, 1922. The only family members she had left were her brothers

Albert and Harry, and a niece, Beatrice Brown. Beatrice was with Nellie during her last days. Nellie willed her a pearl necklace and an octagon platinum ring. She left Harry her diamond earrings, but most of her estate went to Oscar Bondy. Her estate consisted of Austrian money in her safe deposit box, her stock in the American Sugar Refining Company, her deposits in the Union Dime Savings Bank, and a "Victoria broach given to the House of Belgium by the Queen herself."

It had been a long time since Nellie made headlines with her trip around the world. Most people had forgotten her name, but the reforms she had fought for and the opportunities for women she had created would have a lasting impact on American life. They continue to this day, as does her fame as a newspaper reporter. The *Journal* mourned her passing with these simple words: "She was considered the best reporter in America."

Selected Bibliography

Baker, Nina Brown. *Nellie Bly, Reporter*. New York: Holt, Rinehart & Winston, 1956.

Bergman, Carol and Murial Nussbaum. "Nellie Bly." *American History Illustrated* (March 1987), 22-26, 35.

Bettmann, Otto L. *The Good Old Days—They Were Terrible!* New York: Random House, 1974.

Bisland, Elizabeth. "A Flying Trip Around the World." *Cosmopolitan* 8 (1889-1890), 691-700.

_____. "A Flying Trip Around the World." *Cosmopolitan* 9 (1890), 51-60, 173-184, 273-284, 401-413, 533-545, 666-677.

Bly, Nellie. *Nellie Bly's Book: Around the World in 72 Days*. New York: Pictoral Weeklies Company, 1890.

_____. *Six Months in Mexico*. New York: American Publishers Corp., 1888.

Brown, Lea Ann. "Elizabeth Cochrane" in *Dictionary of Literary Biography*, Vol. 25. Detroit: Gale Research, 1984.

Hahn, Emily. *Around the World with Nellie Bly.* Boston: Houghton Mifflin, 1959.

Lorant, Stefan. *Pittsburgh, The Story of an American City.* New York: Doubleday, 1964.

Noble, Iris. *Nellie Bly: First Woman Reporter.* New York: Julian Messner, 1956.

Rittenhouse, Mignon. *The Amazing Nellie Bly.* Freeport, NY: Books for Libraries Press, 1971.

Ross, Ishbel. *Charmers & Cranks.* New York: Harper & Row, 1965.

_____. *Ladies of the Press.* New York: Harper & Brothers, 1936.

Willard, Frances E. and Mary A. Livermore, eds. *A Woman of the Century.* 1893. Reprint. Detroit: Gale Research, 1967.

/ Index